THE UNITE[AN
NUCLEAR DISARMAMEN I

Achievements on the Way to a Nuclear-Weapon-Free World

Information Guide for Photo Exhibition

by
William Epstein

997

NOTE

The Centre for Disarmament Affairs is publishing this information guide to the photo exhibition "The United Nations and Nuclear Disarmament" in collaboration with Fusen Heshi no Kai (Veterans Against War, Japan), Franciscans International, Veterans for Peace (USA) and the NGO Committee on Disarmament, Inc., within the mandate of the United Nations Disarmament Information Programme (UNDIP).

William Epstein, former Director of Disarmament Affairs at the United Nations, was the consultant to the project and author of the *Information Guide*.

Photo credits:
United Nations Photo Library
United Nations Archives
Bettman Archive
Presidential Libraries and Archives

Photo research and collection:
Kan Akatani (Fusen Heshi no Kai)
William Epstein (Consultant)
Benjamin Weintraub (Veterans for Peace, USA)

Exhibition photos printed by:
Robert Del Tredici (Canada)

The views expressed herein are those of the author and do not necessarily reflect those of the United Nations.

The Photo Exhibition was opened on 22 October 1997
United Nations, New York

THE UNITED NATIONS AND NUCLEAR DISARMAMENT

Achievements on the Way to a Nuclear-Weapon-Free World

Information Guide For Photo Exhibition

by
William Epstein

Contents

THE UNITED NATIONS AND NUCLEAR DISARMAMENT

Achievements on the Way to a Nuclear-Weapon-Free World

Information Guide For Photo Exhibition

by
William Epstein

Introduction

This booklet was prepared to give the viewers of the Photographic Exhibition on the United Nations and Nuclear Disarmament the background history and a brief outline of the progress made in the field of nuclear disarmament by the efforts of the United Nations.

The exhibition, and therefore this booklet, concentrate almost solely on nuclear weapons. This is because nuclear weapons are unique. While chemical and biological weapons are horrendous weapons of mass destruction which have been threats for centuries, only nuclear weapons can destroy our civilization and world, and are thus the most destructive weapons ever invented. They have changed all the rules of conduct of international affairs in both peace and war. Not only was the atomic bomb immediately recognized as the decisive weapon of war, it was also clear that international affairs and the relations between the great powers and between atomic and non-atomic powers would never be the same again, and that they would develop in ways that remain undefined.

The exhibition was conceived to provide a visual demonstration of the progress made in the persistent and sustained efforts of the international community to rid the world of the threat of nuclear weapons.

Progress towards the goal of the elimination of nuclear weapons sometimes appears to be slow, painfully slow, and during the early years of the Cold War, practically non-existent.

Nevertheless, the efforts to contain the nuclear arms race, and to halt and reverse it, have been pursued from the earliest days of the United Nations to the present time. Some people have said that the history of nuclear disarmament in the past half century has been a sorry record of failure in the light of the needs; others have said that it was a splendid record of achievement in the light of the obstacles. Both views are probably right, but a final verdict is not yet possible.

This exhibition is intended to highlight the main successes and achievements in the long and continuing efforts to prevent a nuclear war, and to help to inspire and stimulate even greater efforts to nuclear disarmament and ultimately to achieve the goal of a nuclear-weapon-free world.

Birth of the Nuclear Age

The nuclear age began on 16 July 1945 with the explosion of the Trinity atom bomb at Alamagordo, New Mexico. The atom bomb was conceived and born in war as the ultimate weapon of war.

The peaceful applications of atomic energy were also perceived as having great potential in industry, medicine, and agriculture and above all as a new source for the generation of cheap electric power. Unfortunately, for much of the time military considerations far outweighed the peaceful uses. Indeed, the invention of this awesome weapon led to the quantitative and qualitative development of what was called the absolute weapon, such as the world had never seen or ever dreamed would happen.

The hydrogen bomb, capable of an explosion more than 1,000 times the power of the atomic bomb, was invented in 1952. It was called a "thermonuclear" bomb, and in due course the name of "nuclear" bomb was adopted to cover both the atomic bomb, whose energy came from the fission of atoms, and the hydrogen bomb, whose energy came from the fusion of atoms.

During the Cold War when the nuclear arms race was at its hottest, it is estimated that the nuclear stockpiles numbered somewhere between 70,000 and 100,000 warheads with almost 98% held by the two superpowers, the U.S. and the U.S.S.R. The enormity of this stockpile was estimated to be at least 100 times greater than needed to deter an enemy, and led to the coining of the term "overkill".

Role of the United Nations

The Charter of the United Nations was signed in San Francisco, on 25 June 1945, just three weeks before the explosion of the Trinity atom bomb. Since work on the atom bomb was carried on in the greatest secrecy in the Manhattan Project, the Charter made no reference either to the bomb or atomic energy.

Nevertheless, the provisions of the Charter dealing with disarmament and the regulation of armaments as ways to promote international peace and security were more than adequate to deal with all aspects of the problem of disarmament including nuclear weapons and nuclear energy. Indeed the United Nations was seen as the natural and logical agency to do so.

The first meeting of the General Assembly of the United Nations was convened in London on 10 January 1946 and the first meeting of the Security Council on 17 January 1946. The five permanent members of the Security Council (China, France, the Soviet Union, the United Kingdom and the United States—who are known as the P-5) and Canada (which had been involved with the United States and the United Kingdom in the work leading to the invention of the atomic bomb) jointly proposed a draft resolution in the General Assembly for the "establishment of a Commission to deal with problems raised by the discovery of atomic energy". The resolution was adopted unanimously by the then 51 members of the United Nations on 24 January 1946 as Resolution 1 (I) signifying that it was the first resolution of the first General Assembly. (See the text of the resolution in Annex 1)

The UN Atomic Energy Commission was composed of the states

members of the Security Council and Canada and it was to work under the Security Council. The Commission's main tasks were to make recommendations "for the control of atomic energy to ensure its use only for peaceful purposes", and "for the elimination from national armaments of atomic weapons" and of all other weapons of mass destruction.

The plan proposed by the United States in 1946, known as the "Baruch Plan", called for a UN Commission to own, manage and control all atomic energy; it was approved by the UN Atomic Energy Commission. A plan for a census of conventional armaments and forces was also approved by the Commission for Conventional Armaments that was established by the UN Security Council to deal with these weapons. In the meantime the Soviet Union was working on its own atomic bomb, and exploded its first one in September 1949. The Soviet Union vetoed both plans when they were sent to the Security Council because of its completely different approach to disarmament from that of the United States and its allies; it wanted to ban the bomb immediately and destroy all bombs within three months.

In an effort to solve the deadlock, the two Commissions were merged into a new Disarmament Commission in 1952. At first the Disarmament Commission was also composed of the members of the Security Council plus Canada but, in 1958, the General Assembly enlarged it to include all members of the United Nations.

Years of Deadlock

Because of the Cold War, however, a nuclear arms race between the two superpowers—the United States and the USSR—had spread to the other permanent members of the Security Council (the P-5). The United Kingdom in 1952, France in 1960 and China in 1964 had exploded their own first atom bombs, so that all of the P-5 were by 1964 recognized as nuclear powers.

The two superpowers, however, were very much the main actors in the development of nuclear weapons. At their peak, they possessed a total of some 70,000 ready nuclear weapons, while the

4

other three nuclear powers possessed between them 1,000 to 1,500 in all.

For the first 15 years or so of the Cold War all the persistent UN efforts remained deadlocked and failed to halt or slow down the nuclear arms race. At the same time there were growing fears of the spread of nuclear weapons to additional countries. It seemed clear that, so long as any nuclear power believed that it needed nuclear weapons for its security, whether for deterrence or for seeking or maintaining nuclear superiority, other countries would also seek to acquire them for their own security and not just the P-5 powers.

In 1959 Chairman Nikita Khruschev of the Soviet Union came to the United Nations and proposed a plan to achieve general and complete disarmament that would include nuclear and other weapons of mass destruction (biological and chemical weapons) and also conventional weapons. Mr. Khruschev urged that his plan would overcome the obstacles regarding questions of control, and also over the priorities concerning nuclear and conventional disarmament, since it provided for complete control over complete disarmament. His proposal was adopted unanimously by the General Assembly which considered "the question of general and complete disarmament is the most important one facing the world today" and called on "Governments to achieve a constructive solution of this problem", and that necessary measures leading toward that goal should be agreed in the shortest possible time. It also requested the UN Disarmament Commission and the Ten-Nation Committee on Disarmament (which consisted of five leading Western and Eastern powers and which had been established in 1959 at a meeting of France, the Soviet Union, the United Kingdom and the United States) to give thorough consideration to all proposals made in the General Assembly on the question of general and complete disarmament.

The deadlock between East and West continued all during 1960, but in the summer of 1961 the Soviet Union and the United States undertook an exchange of views on the best way to proceed with negotiations on disarmament. The exchange of views was conducted by John J. McCloy of the United States and Valerian A. Zorin of

5

the Soviet Union in Washington, Moscow and New York in June, July and September and resulted in a statement of agreed principles for multilateral negotiations on disarmament which have come to be known as the McCloy-Zorin Agreed Principles or, more formally, as the Soviet Union-United States Joint Statement of Agreed Principles for Disarmament Negotiations. The Agreed Principles constitute an important breakthrough in the years of deadlock and it is set out in Annex 2 hereto.

On 29 December 1961, the General Assembly unanimously adopted a draft resolution submitted jointly by the Soviet Union and the United States which approved the Joint Statement of Agreed Principles and recommended that they should be the basis for negotiations on general and complete disarmament. It also approved a new Eighteen-Nation Disarmament Committee (ENDC) composed of five leading states from each of the East and West and eight non-aligned countries: Brazil, Burma, Ethiopia, India, Mexico, Nigeria, Sweden and the United Arab Republic (Egypt), to undertake the negotiations and to report to the Disarmament Commission and the General Assembly.

Years of Achievement

The Joint Statement of Agreed Principles and the establishment of the ENDC (the predecessor of what eventually became the current 61-member Conference on Disarmament) constitute a turning point in the disarmament negotiations. The years of deadlock were ended and succeeded by years of achievement of disarmament agreements and treaties. While the Cold War and the nuclear arms race continued, a period of detente (reduction of tensions) developed in the 1960's and 1970's.

The McCloy-Zorin Principles made it possible for the members of the ENDC to consider both general and complete disarmament and also collateral measures of partial disarmament that could be an integral part of the larger framework of general and complete disarmament. At its very beginning the ENDC had for its consideration a Soviet Draft Treaty on General and Complete Disarmament Under Strict International Control and a United States Out-

6

line of Basic Provisions of a Treaty on General and Complete Disarmament in a Peaceful World.

The discussion of these two draft treaties on general and complete disarmament quickly reached an impasse and, on the initiative of the eight non-aligned countries, the ENDC turned its attention to banning nuclear weapon testing as a collateral partial measure that they considered to be the first step to nuclear disarmament.

Banning Nuclear Testing

Prime Minister Jawaharlal Nehru of India made the first proposal for the suspension of nuclear weapon testing in April 1954 after the dangerous radioactive fall-out from testing hydrogen bombs in the Pacific Ocean. It quickly became the measure of nuclear disarmament most favored by the non-nuclear states, and more time and attention over the years was devoted to efforts to stop nuclear testing than to any other issue of nuclear disarmament. In the latter part of the 1950s and early 1960s, the then three nuclear powers—the United States, the Soviet Union and the United Kingdom—carried on a series of negotiations for the discontinuance of nuclear tests and encouraging progress was made. These were continued in the ENDC which devoted a special session to that item, in November-December 1962, and it was the principal subject in the resumed ENDC session in 1963.

The main obstacle to agreement was over the question of the verification of a ban on underground testing in order to be able to distinguish an underground test from an earthquake. At one time it seemed that agreement was within reach when the United States said it could accept seven on-site inspections per year of underground seismic events to make sure that they were not nuclear explosions. The Soviet Union offered to accept three-on-site inspections per year. The three African non-aligned countries proposed a compromise of "three, four or so" inspections a year or an adequately proportionate figure spread over more years. There was a generally held belief among many of the non-nuclear states that the three nuclear powers could have accepted any of the three proposals without any sacrifice of their security, but that it suited the purposes of the three nuclear powers not to reach any agreement to end all testing.

Finally, however, in the aftermath of the Cuban missile crisis in October 1962, the Soviet Union agreed to accept one alternative that the United States and United Kingdom had offered on several previous occasions and which the General Assembly had approved in 1962, but which the Soviet Union had repeatedly rejected, namely, to ban only tests in the atmosphere, in outer space and under water, as these tests (unlike underground ones) could easily be detected without any international means of verification.

The three nuclear powers—The Soviet Union, the United Kingdom and the United States—met in Moscow on 15 July 1963 and quickly reached agreement on the Treaty Banning Nuclear Tests in the Atmosphere, in Outer Space and Under Water, known as the *Partial Test Ban Treaty* (PTBT), which was signed in Moscow on 5 August 1963 by the Foreign Ministers of the three countries.

The Treaty, which was open to all states for signature and which contained a pledge in the preamble stating that the parties were determined to continue negotiations to discontinue all testing of nuclear weapons for all time, was heralded as the first great achievement of a treaty on nuclear disarmament. It entered into force on 10 October 1963 and it was noted with approval and satisfaction by the General Assembly in November 1963. The General Assembly also requested the ENDC to continue its negotiations to achieve the discontinuance of all tests of nuclear weapons. The Treaty has more than 120 parties. China and France had not formally joined the Treaty but voluntarily stopped testing in those environments. When the Nuclear Non-Proliferation Treaty (NPT) was being negotiated, the non-nuclear countries succeeded in including in its preamble the promise of the nuclear powers to continue negotiations to end all nuclear weapon tests.

Subsequent attempts to achieve a comprehensive test ban treaty (CTBT), however, constitute a long and tortuous history, with the nuclear powers unwilling for one reason or another to conduct serious negotiations for a total test ban. Since the nuclear powers continued to conduct underground tests at a greater rate than they had previously conducted tests in the atmosphere, the PTBT became more of a health and environmental treaty than a measure of nuclear disarmament.

Eventually, out of sheer frustration, a group of non-aligned states, led by Mexico, decided to take advantage of the amendment provisions of the PTBT and called on the three depository States (the Soviet Union, the United Kingdom and the United States) to convene a conference of the parties to amend the treaty by banning underground tests. The General Assembly supported the amendment procedure and the convening of the conference.

The Test Ban Amendment Conference convened in January 1991. The United Kingdom and the United States opposed any amendment without an effective verification system and indicated that they would exercise their veto rights to prevent its entering into force. The conference decided, however, to continue in being and to reconvene when its President considered the time was appropriate.

On 10 August 1993, the Conference on Disarmament finally decided to give its Nuclear Test Ban Committee a mandate to negotiate a comprehensive test ban treaty (CTBT). On the same day, a special meeting convened by the President of the Amendment Conference at the United Nations of the parties to the PTBT decided that the work on a CTBT in the Amendment Conference and in the Conference on Disarmament should be mutually supportive and complementary and that the President of the Amendment Conference should continue his consultations and decide when the Amendment Conference should meet again.

Since the Conference on Disarmament began serious negotiations to achieve a CTBT, the leaders of the Amendment Conference considered that they had succeeded in their efforts as the question of a CTBT was now very high on the international agenda. Indeed, at the 1995 NPT Review and Extension Conference the five nuclear-weapon states agreed with the other parties to the NPT that the Conference on Disarmament would complete its negotiations on a CTBT "no later than 1996". Despite nearly three years of intensive efforts, the Conference on Disarmament found that it could not reach a consensus on the text of a comprehensive test ban treaty. All but one or two members of the Conference on Disarmament supported the text of the treaty prepared by the Chairman of the Committee negotiating the provisions of the treaty, with a detailed system of verification. In order to bring the matter to a successful conclusion in 1996, as agreed by the 1995 NPT Review and Extension Conference, and also to comply with the resolution of the General Assembly at its 50th session later in the same year, Australia brought the text of the treaty to the General Assembly for its adoption. The Australian resolution was co-sponsored by 127 states which ensured its adoption by an overwhelming majority of the General Assembly on 10 September 1996.

India opposed the adoption of the treaty which it considered as flawed, as did a number of countries that nevertheless voted for its adoption. India stated that so long as the nuclear powers refused to agree to eliminate their nuclear arsenals within a fixed time limit, it intended to maintain its option to acquire nuclear weapons. It also declared that it would not sign or ratify the Treaty, although its name was included, despite India's opposition, in the list of 44 countries whose ratification was necessary for the Treaty to enter into force. The list included the five nuclear powers and 39 other countries who were considered to have the capability to manufacture nuclear weapons if they so chose.

The Treaty was opened for signature on 24 September 1996. All five nuclear powers signed on the first day, as did 66 other states, and currently the total exceeds 140 signatories.

Despite the problem that remains about its entry into force, the Treaty is generally considered as a very important achievement. Successive Secretaries-General of the UN have described a nuclear test ban as a "litmus test" of the intentions of the nuclear powers to pursue nuclear disarmament. It is regarded as the first step toward the elimination of nuclear weapons. The signature of the Treaty ensures that there will be no more nuclear test explosions until some way is found for its entry into force. Perhaps most important is that it revives the hopes and dreams that the world community has finally taken the first necessary step to rid the world of nuclear weapons.

Preventing the Spread of Nuclear Weapons

From the beginning of the nuclear age all countries agreed, as did the United Nations, that the proliferation of nuclear weapons posed the greatest threat to humanity, and that nuclear weapons should be eliminated under adequate safeguards. When it was clear that the goal of eliminating nuclear weapons was not going to be achieved during the Cold War, the efforts of the world community turned to reducing the risks and dangers of the continued proliferation of these weapons by the nuclear powers and to prevent their spreading to additional countries. After the failure of the Baruch Plan and the efforts of the UN's Atomic Energy Commission, the UN's efforts turned (as we have discussed in the previous section) to banning nuclear testing which is not only an important way to prevent the proliferation of nuclear weapons but is also considered to be the first step on the way to nuclear disarmament.

The International Atomic Energy Agency (IAEA)

In 1953, President Dwight D. Eisenhower of the United States made his "Atoms for Peace" proposal to the U.N. General Assembly. Since it was very difficult to achieve nuclear disarmament by the direct approach of eliminating nuclear weapons, he considered that it could best be promoted by the indirect approach of building up the peaceful uses of atomic energy under effective safeguards to ensure that it was not diverted to building nuclear weapons. He proposed that the nuclear powers should contribute fissionable material for such peaceful uses to an agency of the UN to help other countries to obtain the benefits of atomic energy. This could be done without setting up a complete world-wide system of inspection and control. This proposal led to creation of the *International Atomic Energy Agency (IAEA)*, whose task is to promote the peaceful uses of atomic energy under a system of IAEA safeguards.

The Outer Space Treaty

In 1963, the General Assembly unanimously adopted a resolution to ban nuclear and other weapons of mass destruction from outer space. After negotiations, the Soviet Union and the United States reached agreement on a "Treaty on Principles Governing the Activities of States in the Exploration and Use of Outer Space including the Moon and other Celestial Bodies", which is known as the *Outer Space Treaty.* It was unanimously endorsed by the General Assembly in 1966 and was opened for signature in January 1967. In Article IV, the parties agreed not to place in orbit any nuclear or other weapons of mass destruction, or install them on celestial bodies or station them in outer space. The moon and other celestial bodies were to be used solely for peaceful purposes; military bases and installations and the testing of any type of weapon and military maneuvers were prohibited. The Treaty recognized the common interest in the use of outer space for peaceful purposes and ensured that outer space would be a nuclear-free and disarmed area.

The Treaty of Tlatelolco Creates the First Nuclear-Weapon-Free Zone (NWFZ)

The Cuban Missile Crisis of October 1962 brought the nations of the world to the brink of the nuclear abyss. The governments and people of Latin America decided that they should never again be subjected to the threats and fears of a nuclear war. On 29 April 1963 the Presidents of five Latin American Republics issued a declaration on the denuclearization of Latin America. This was followed by a resolution of the General Assembly in November 1963 supporting the Latin American states' efforts for denuclearization, and calling for the co-operation of all states, particularly the nuclear powers, and the UN Secretary-General.

On the initiative of Mexico a meeting was held in Mexico City in November 1964 that established a Preparatory Commission for the Denuclearization of Latin America. Negotiations continued until a draft treaty was agreed by the members of the Commission to cover all the states of Latin America and the Caribbean. The Treaty for the Prohibition of Nuclear Weapons in Latin America was signed in the borough of Tlatelolco in Mexico City (from which it gets its name as the *Treaty of Tlatelolco*) on 14 February 1967.

The Treaty was hailed for creating for the first time in history a NWFZ in an inhabited part of the earth, and also as the first treaty that established a system of control and safeguards under a permanent supervisory organ and with the assistance of the IAEA.

The Treaty prohibited the testing, use, manufacture, production or acquisition by any means whatsoever of nuclear weapons by the parties, and also the receipt, storage, installation, deployment and any form of possession of nuclear weapons in the zone. A Protocol to the Treaty bound the five nuclear powers to fully respect and not in any way violate the Treaty and also not to use or threaten to use nuclear weapons against the parties to the Treaty. By 1979 all five nuclear powers had ratified the Protocol, thus making this the first treaty which placed meaningful restrictions and limitations on the stationing, deployment, use and threat of use of their nuclear weapons by the nuclear powers.

The Treaty of Tlatelolco became a model for similar nuclear-weapon-free-zones in other parts of the world. In August 1985 the *Treaty of Rarotonga* established a NWFZ for the South Pacific; in December 1995 the *Treaty of Bangkok* established a NWFZ for Southeast Asia was signed in Bangkok; in April 1996 the *Treaty of Pelindaba* establishing a NWFZ for Africa was signed in Cairo.

There are current proposals for several other NWFZ treaties for other parts of the world. The continued creation of such zones with undertakings by the nuclear powers to fully respect them constitutes an important way to contain and prevent the spread of nuclear weapons.

Treaty on the Non-Proliferation of Nuclear Weapons (NPT)

The Treaty commonly known as the "*Non-Proliferation Treaty*" (NPT) is the corner-stone of the international structure to prevent the proliferation of nuclear weapons. After years of negotiations in the ENDC it was signed in July 1968 and entered into force in 1970. It has more than 180 parties, including the five declared nuclear powers, more than any other disarmament treaty. It is set out in Annex 3 hereto.

The idea of preventing the further spread of nuclear weapons was first introduced in the General Assembly by Ireland in 1958. After France in 1960 and China in 1964 exploded their first atomic bombs, and after the conclusion of the Partial Test Ban Treaty in 1963, the General Assembly turned its attention to nuclear non-proliferation. Intensive negotiations were pursued in the ENDC from 1965 to 1968 led by the United States and the Soviet Union. Their first draft treaties submitted in the ENDC aimed only at preventing "horizontal proliferation", i.e. the spread of nuclear weapons to additional countries. The first provision dealt with the undertaking by the participating nuclear powers not to transfer nuclear weapons or explosive devices or control over them to any recipient or to help any non-nuclear state to manufacture or acquire control over them; there was little likelihood that they would do so in any case. The second provision dealt with the undertaking by the non-nuclear states not to receive such weapons from any transferor and not to manufacture or acquire them or receive assistance to do so.

The eight non-aligned members of the ENDC, however, insisted that the treaty must also prevent "vertical proliferation", i.e. the further testing, production and deployment of nuclear weapons by the nuclear powers.

The nuclear powers also wanted a system of IAEA safeguards to ensure that the non-nuclear states were abiding by their undertakings. The non-nuclear countries for their part wanted security assurances that they would not be subject to the use or threat of use of nuclear weapons, and that they would receive assistance in the peaceful uses of nuclear energy.

After lengthy negotiations the nuclear powers agreed in Article VI of the Treaty that they would pursue negotiations in good faith (a) for the cessation of the nuclear arms race at an early date, (b) for nuclear disarmament, and (c) on a treaty on general and complete disarmament. They also agreed to provide some security assurances by declarations and a resolution for that purpose in the UN Security Council, and for some measure of accountability by review conferences every five years to ensure that the purposes of the preamble and the provisions of the Treaty were being realized.

In addition, after 25 years a conference of the parties would be held to decide on the extension of the Treaty, and any party could withdraw from the Treaty on three months notice if extraordinary events had jeopardized its supreme interests.

The NPT entered into force in 1970 and review conferences were held every five years beginning in 1975. Final declarations were agreed by consensus in 1975 and 1985 but, because of differences among the parties as to whether the nuclear powers had lived up to their obligations under the Treaty, most notably Article VI, no consensus on a final declaration could be reached in 1980, 1990 and 1995.

Nevertheless, at the NPT Review and Extension Conference held in 1995, the parties agreed without a vote to three decisions:

(1) to strengthen the review process of the Treaty by providing for greater accountability,

(2) On a set of 20 principles and objectives for nuclear nonproliferation and disarmament which took into account some of the main concerns of the non-nuclear states, including a program of action under Article VI of the NPT which provided for (a) the conclusion of a comprehensive test ban treaty "no later than 1996", (b) an early ban on the production of fissile material for weapons, and (c) the determined pursuit by the nuclear powers of systematic and progressive efforts to reduce nuclear weapons with the ultimate goal of eliminating them and by all states of general and complete disarmament;

(3) to extend the NPT indefinitely.

The nuclear powers and their allies were greatly pleased by the indefinite extension of the Treaty, and the fact that most of the non-aligned parties supported such a decision. Some of the non-aligned, however, made it clear that they would have preferred a series of 25 year extensions. Under the decision to strengthen the review process, Preparatory Committee meetings, the first of which would be held in 1997, will be convened each year thereafter, for the review conference in the year 2,000.

Nuclear Disarmament
and the American-Soviet Summit Meetings
SALT I Agreements

After the failure of the United States sponsored "Baruch Plan" in the UN Atomic Energy Commission, and the difficulties encountered in the ENDC concerning the negotiation of a treaty on general and complete disarmament, efforts to deal directly with the reduction of the nuclear arsenals were in abeyance. After the signature in July 1968 of the NPT, however, in an effort to begin implementing Article VI of that Treaty, the United States and the USSR, the two superpowers, began direct bilateral negotiations on nuclear disarmament. They were cautiously called the Strategic Arms Limitation Talks (SALT) and were intended to discuss the limitation of both strategic nuclear weapon delivery systems (the name given to inter-continental ballistic missiles (ICBMs) that could reach each other's territory) and defenses against ballistic missiles whose development and deployment were at an early stage. After two and one-half years of negotiations, two accords were reached in Moscow in May 1972 at a summit meeting between General Secretary Leonid Brezhnev and President Richard Nixon. The *Treaty on the Limitation of Anti-Ballistic Missiles (ABM Treaty)*, which is of unlimited duration, permits each side to have one limited ABM system to protect its capital and another one to protect its ICBM launch area. Each site could have up to 100 launchers and 100 interceptor missiles, with each launcher capable of launching only one interceptor missile at a time. Each party also agreed not to develop, test or deploy ABM systems that are sea-based, air-based, space-based or mobile land-based. (Subsequently, the ABM Treaty was amended by a Protocol in July 1974 which limited each side to one ABM deployment site). The Treaty established the policy of equal security through mutual vulnerability.

The second accord signed in May 1972, was the Interim Agreement on the Limitation of Offensive Arms, known as the *"Interim Agreement"*, which was to last for five years, to freeze the number of land-based ICBM launchers and submarine-launched ballistic missile (SLBM) launchers to the numbers already deployed and under construction. Thus the Soviet Union could have 1618 ICBMs and 950 SLBMs on 62 submarines, and the United States 1054 ICBMs and 710 SLBMs on 44 submarines.

Each of the two agreements relied only on national technical means for verification of compliance, but a Standing Consultative Commission was established that would deal with questions of compliance and other problems that might arise.

During the course of the bilateral negotiations, their progress was followed and discussed both in the ENDC's enlarged successor negotiating body in Geneva and by the General Assembly which encouraged the bilateral negotiations and urged more rapid progress. Both the United States and the Soviet Union stressed that the two agreements were a concrete expression of their carrying out of their obligations under Article VI of the NPT. The General Assembly noted the agreements with satisfaction and urged the two governments to expedite further agreements and to keep the General Assembly informed of further progress.

During the decade of the 1970's, there were several other bilateral agreements on reducing the risk of the outbreak of nuclear war, and at summit meetings in Washington in 1973 and in Vladivostok in 1974, which dealt with various aspects of the negotiations and the signature in 1973 of an Agreement on the Prevention of Nuclear War. The decade of the 1970's was regarded as a period of developing detente between the two superpowers.

In June 1979, they signed the SALT II Treaty in Vienna which provided for actual reductions in the number of strategic delivery vehicles and, for the first time, dealt with the long-range bombers and with launchers of ICBMs and SLBMs equipped with Multiple Independently Targeted Re-entry Vehicles (MIRVs), which were delivery vehicles that carried several warheads. However the SALT II Treaty was never ratified although both parties declared they would abide by it. The new United States Administration under President Ronald Reagan was critical of the SALT II Treaty and proposed a new approach to negotiations which it called the Strategic Arms Reduction Talks (START). The new START negotiations began in Geneva in June 1982.

Gorbachev-Reagan Summit Meetings

When the new administration took over in the U.S. in 1981, the period of developing detente underwent a change. The early 1980's saw a build-up of military weapons by the two superpowers and a hardening of the rhetoric in their public statements. The new START negotiations showed little progress and were suspended between 1983 and 1985. In 1983 President Reagan launched his Strategic Defense Initiative (SDI, popularly known as "Star Wars") to develop an effective defense against all strategic (meaning long-range) nuclear missiles. This initiative added a new dimension to the race for missile defenses and for ways of countering them. Also during this period, both the Soviet Union and the United States began deploying new intermediate range nuclear ballistic missiles and cruise missiles which brought about a qualitative and quantitative change of the security situation in Europe.

When Mikhail Gorbachev became General Secretary of the Central Committee of the Communist Party and the new leader of the Soviet Union in 1985, he adopted a new policy of openness (glasnost) and began to change the entire rhetoric concerning East-West relations.

In November 1985 the first of a new series of Soviet-U.S. summit meetings was held in Geneva between Gorbachev and Reagan. For the first time they announced that they were agreed that "a nuclear war cannot be won and must never be fought". This dramatic statement was re-affirmed at four subsequent summit meetings of the two leaders—at Reykjavik (1986), Washington (1987), and at Moscow and New York (1988).

At the Geneva summit meeting they also agreed on the principle of 50% reductions in their nuclear arsenals and for an interim accord on intermediate-range nuclear forces.

At the Reykjavik summit meeting in October 1986, the process was carried forward although no agreement was concluded. However, both sides seriously discussed and seemed to be close to agreement on the elimination of all strategic nuclear ballistic missiles in 10 years—that is by the end of 1996—and for an interim agreement on the drastic reduction (and possible elimination from Europe) of all intermediate-range nuclear weapons. No final agreement could be reached, however, as the Soviet Union insisted that the SDI program of the U.S. should in effect be abandoned, which the U.S. was unwilling to do.

The INF Treaty

Nevertheless, the summit meetings at Geneva and Reykjavik did lead to an important breakthrough in the long history of nuclear disarmament efforts. At their third summit meeting in December 1987 in Washington, President Reagan and General Secretary Gorbachev signed the *Treaty on the Elimination of Their Intermediate-Range and Shorter-Range Missiles*, commonly known as the *INF Treaty* (Intermediate-Range Nuclear Forces).

This historic agreement provided for the elimination and destruction of all land-based (ground-launched) nuclear ballistic missiles and cruise missiles of the two superpowers with ranges between 500 and 5500 kilometers. This was the first time in the history of the nuclear age that a whole class of nuclear weapons was totally abolished worldwide. It also provided for an intrusive system of verification and on-site inspection. It did not abolish air- or sea-launched ballistic or cruise missiles, or long-range (strategic) missiles with a range over 5500 kilometers, or short-range (tactical) nuclear weapons with ranges up to 500 kilometers. However, it marked a turning point in American-Soviet and in Soviet-European relations.

The START I Treaty

The changing political and military climate, the dissolution of the Warsaw Pact and the end of the Cold War made it possible for the Soviet Union and the United States to conclude the first *Strate-*

gic Arms Reduction Treaty (START I) which applied to long range (over 5500 kilometers) weapons. It was signed in Moscow in July 1991 by President George Bush and General Secretary Mikhail Gorbachev.

The Treaty provides that each side would reduce its strategic weapons to a total number of 1600 nuclear delivery vehicles—intercontinental ballistic missiles (ICBMs), submarine-launched ballistic missiles (SLBMs) and heavy bombers. These 1600 delivery vehicles could carry no more than a total of 6000 nuclear warheads. These limits were to be met over a period of seven years, and were subject to a strict verification regime including on-site inspections. The Treaty is the first disarmament treaty that reduced strategic nuclear weapons by both superpowers, and by almost one-third.

During September and October 1991, George Bush and Mikhail Gorbachev announced further unilateral reductions of short-range (tactical) nuclear weapons and ending the development of new mobile ICBMs.

After the dissolution of the Soviet Union at the end of 1991, Russia became the main successor state with Boris Yeltsin as its President, and the former republics of the Soviet Union became members of the Commonwealth of Independent States (CIS). In May 1992, the *Lisbon Protocol* was signed by the United States, Russia, Belarus, Kazakhstan and Ukraine, making all five states parties to the START I Treaty. Belarus, Kazakhstan and Ukraine agreed to transfer all their nuclear weapons to Russia and to eliminate them from their territories. They also acceded to and became parties to the Nuclear Non-Proliferation Treaty.

The START II Treaty

Because it took some time for the three new parties to the START I Treaty to ratify it, it did not enter into force until 1994. Nevertheless, negotiations for further reductions of their strategic nuclear forces led to the signing in Moscow by President George Bush and President Boris Yeltsin of the START II Treaty on 3 January 1993.

Under the START II Treaty, the United States and Russia agreed to reduce their deployed strategic nuclear warheads to 3000 and 3500 each by 1 January 2003. They also agreed to eliminate all multiple warhead ICBMs and limited the number of warheads on SLBMs to 1750. At the time of writing, the START II Treaty had not yet entered into force, but both parties have agreed that they will begin negotiations for further reductions in a START III Treaty as soon as the START II Treaty enters into force. They also agreed at a summit meeting in Helsinki in March 1997 that START III will establish by December 31, 2007 a ceiling of 2,000-2,500 strategic nuclear weapons for each country. For the first time, the START III Treaty would include measures to promote the irreversibility of the deep reductions by transparency regarding nuclear warhead inventories and by the destruction of strategic nuclear warheads.

The First U.N. Special Session on Disarmament (SSOD I)

In 1969, the General Assembly proclaimed the 1970's as the First Disarmament Decade and called on governments to intensify their efforts to achieve the cessation of the nuclear arms race, nuclear disarmament and a treaty on general and complete disarmament. It also wanted to strengthen the role of the U.N. in multilateral disarmament matters. In 1976, on the initiative of the non-aligned countries which was widely supported, the General Assembly decided to hold a special session on disarmament (SSOD). It was clear that there had not been sufficient progress to halt the arms race in both nuclear and conventional weapons. Military expenditures were increasing and there was a general feeling that despite the various partial agreements in the field of disarmament, a new approach was needed as well as a global strategy for future disarmament.

SSOD I was held at the U.N. in May & June 1978 and it was the largest and most representative meeting ever held to consider disarmament, with many heads of government, foreign ministers and other high officials participating actively and presenting many new ideas and proposals. For the first time in the history of disarmament, a consensus was reached on the Final Document which contained a Declaration of Principles, a Programme of Action, and

Machinery for Disarmament.

The Final Document emphasized the principles of the central role and primary responsibility of the U.N. in the field of disarmament, the absolute necessity of success in disarmament if humanity is to survive, and the best way to achieve the goals of disarmament and peace.

It stated that the "Priorities in disarmament negotiations shall be: nuclear weapons; other weapons of mass destruction, including chemical weapons; conventional weapons including any which may be deemed to be excessively injurious or to have indiscriminate effects; and reduction of armed forces."

In the program of action for nuclear disarmament, it called for agreements to end the qualitative improvement of nuclear weapon systems, an end to the production of nuclear weapons and their delivery vehicles, and for a comprehensive program for progressive reduction of nuclear weapons leading to their ultimate and complete elimination at the earliest possible time.

It also approved the current machinery for disarmament, namely, the First Committee of the General Assembly, the Disarmament Commission, and the Conference on Disarmament as the single multilateral disarmament negotiating forum.

Most members of the United Nations regard the Final Document of SSOD I as the "charter of disarmament" to this day. SSOD II held in 1982 and SSOD III held in 1988 reaffirmed the continued validity of the 1978 Final Document even though they could not adopt any new substantive final document of their own because of the lack of consensus. Negotiations are now proceeding in the United Nations to have another special session (SSOD IV) before the end of the 20th century.

The Advisory Opinion
of the International Court of Justice on the Legality
of the Threat or Use of Nuclear Weapons

The International Court of Justice (commonly referred to as the "World Court"), which has its seat at the Hague in the Netherlands, issued an Advisory Opinion on 8 July 1996 on the "Legality of the Threat or Use of Nuclear Weapons". The Advisory Opinion was issued in response to a request from the UN General Assembly on the question: "Is the threat or use of nuclear weapons in any circumstances permitted under international law?"

The Court, by decision of eight to seven, ruled that the threat or use of nuclear weapons would "generally be contrary to the rules of international law applicable in armed conflict, and in particular the principles and rules of humanitarian law". It added that "the Court cannot conclude definitively whether the threat or use of nuclear weapons would be lawful or unlawful in an extreme circumstance of self-defense, in which the very survival of a State would be at stake".

The Court also decided unanimously that "There exists an obligation to pursue in good faith and bring to a conclusion negotiations leading to nuclear disarmament in all its aspects under strict and effective international control." The Court explained in paragraph 99 of its decision that Article VI of the Nuclear Non-Proliferation Treaty created "an obligation to achieve a precise result— nuclear disarmament in all its aspects—by adopting a particular course of conduct, namely the pursuit of negotiations in good faith". The President of the Court, in casting his deciding vote, stated that since this statement was unanimous, in his view it assumed the force of customary law.

Although advisory opinions are not binding in law, they do enunciate the views of the highest legal authorities in the world and, as such, help to create binding international law. Its decision in this landmark case will have an important effect both on all future discussions and debates on the threat or use of nuclear weapons and also on their elimination.

The Future

With the ending of the Cold War, the goal of eliminating all nuclear arsenals no longer seems to be an impossible dream. Russia and the United States have begun dismantling their huge arsenals of nuclear weapons. China, France and the United Kingdom joined the Nuclear Non-Proliferation Treaty and all five nuclear powers agreed at the 1995 NPT Review and Extension Conference to conclude a comprehensive nuclear test ban treaty in 1996, which they have done. The ban on nuclear testing is generally regarded as the first step on the way to total nuclear disarmament.

At the 1995 NPT conference the five nuclear powers also committed themselves to systematic and progressive efforts to reduce nuclear weapons with the ultimate goal of eliminating them. This can be done either by including China, France and the United Kingdom in the START negotiations, or by beginning negotiations for the elimination of all nuclear weapons at the Conference on Disarmament, which was enlarged in 1996 to 61 member states.

In addition, the Advisory Opinion of the International Court of Justice decided that the nuclear powers that are parties to the Nuclear Non-1.oliferation Treaty have the obligation not only to conduct negotiations in good faith for total nuclear disarmament but also to bring them to a successful conclusion.

Thus, for the first time in the half century since the adoption of General Assembly Resolution 1(I) on 24 January 1946, there is renewed hope that humanity can rid the world of the nuclear threat by achieving its goal of a nuclear-weapon-free world.

ANNEXES

Annex I

General Assembly Resolution 1(I)
of 24 January 1946

ESTABLISHMENT OF A COMMISSION TO DEAL WITH THE PROBLEMS
RAISED BY THE DISCOVERY OF ATOMIC ENERGY

Resolved by the General Assembly of the United Nations to establish a Commission, with the composition and competence set out hereunder, to deal with the problems raised by the discovery of atomic energy and other related matters:

1. Establishment of the Commission
   A Commission is hereby established by the General Assembly with the terms of reference set out under section 5 below.

2. Relations of the Commission with the Organs of the United Nations
   (a) The Commission shall submit its reports and recommendations to the Security Council, and such reports and recommendations shall be made public unless the Security Council, in the interest of peace and security, otherwise directs. In the appropriate cases the Security Council should transmit these reports to the General Assembly and the Members of the United Nations, as well as to the Economic and Social Council and other organs within the framework of the United Nations.
   (b) In view of the Security Council's primary responsibility under the Charter of the United Nations for the maintenance of international peace and security, the Security Council shall issue directions to the Commission in matters affecting security. On these matters the Commission shall be accountable for its work to the Security Council.

3. Composition of the Commission
   The Commission shall be composed of one representative from

each of those States represented on the Security Council, and Canada when that State is not a member of the Security Council. Each representative on the Commission may have such assistance as he may desire.

4. Rules of Procedure

The Commission shall have whatever staff it may deem necessary, and shall make recommendations for its rules of procedure to the Security Council, which shall approve them as a procedural matter.

5. Terms of Reference of the Commission

The Commission shall proceed with the utmost despatch and enquire into all phases of the problem, and make such recommendations from time to time with respect to them as it finds possible. In particular, the Commission shall make specific proposals:

(a) for extending between all nations the exchange of basic scientific information for peaceful ends;

(b) for control of atomic energy to the extent necessary to ensure its use only for peaceful purposes;

(c) for the elimination from national armaments of atomic weapons and of all other major weapons adaptable to mass destruction;

(d) for effective safeguards by way of inspection and other means to protect complying States against the hazards of violations and evasions.

The work of the Commission should proceed by separate stages, the successful completion of each of which will develop the necessary confidence of the world before the next stage is undertaken.

The Commission shall not infringe upon the responsibilities of any organ of the United Nations, but should present recommendations for the consideration of those organs in the performance of their tasks under the terms of the United Nations.

Annex II

The Soviet Union-United States Joint Statement of Agreed Principles for Disarmament Negotiations (McCloy-Zorin Agreed Principles) 20 September 1961

A statement containing agreed principles as a basis for multilateral negotiations on disarmament was issued jointly by the Soviet Union and the United States on 20 September 1961 for circulation to all Members of the United Nations at the sixteenth session. The statement followed an exchange of views between the representatives of the two Governments—at meetings held in Washington, Moscow and New York in June, July and September 1961—on questions relating to disarmament and to the resumption of negotiations on disarmament in an appropriate body.

In the joint statement, the Soviet Union and the United States recommended the following principles as a basis for new negotiations:

1. The goal of negotiations is to achieve agreement on a programme which will ensure:

(a) That disarmament is general and complete and war is no longer an instrument for settling international problems, and

(b) That such disarmament is accompanied by the establishment of reliable procedures for the peaceful settlement of disputes and effective arrangements for the maintenance of peace in accordance with the principles of the Charter of the United Nations.

2. The programme for general and complete disarmament shall ensure that States will have at their disposal only such non-nuclear armaments, forces, facilities and establishments as are agreed to be necessary to maintain internal order and protect the personal security of citizens; and that States shall support and provide agreed manpower for United Nations peace force.

3. To this end, the programme for general and complete disarmament shall contain the necessary provisions, with respect to the military establishment of every nation, for:

(a) The disbanding of armed forces, the dismantling of military establishments, including bases, the cessation of the production of armaments as well as their liquidation or conversion to peaceful uses;

(b) The elimination of all stockpiles of nuclear, chemical, bacteriological and other weapons of mass destruction, and the cessation of the production of such weapons;

(c) The elimination of all means of delivery of weapons of mass destruction;

(d) The abolition of organizations and institutions designed to organize the military effort of States, the cessation of military training, and the closing of all military training institutions;

(e) The discontinuance of military expenditures.

4. The disarmament programme should be implemented in an agreed sequence, by stages, until it is completed, with each measure and stage carried out within specified time-limits. Transition to a subsequent stage in the process of disarmament should take place upon a review of the implementation of measures included in the preceding stage and upon a decision that all such measures have been implemented and verified and that any additional verification arrangements required for measures in the next stage are, when appropriate, ready to operate.

5. All measures of general and complete disarmament should be balanced so that at no stage of the implementation of the treaty could any State or group of States gain military advantage and that security is ensure equally for all.

6. All disarmament measures should be implemented from beginning to end under such strict and effective international control as would provide firm assurance that all parties are honouring their obligations. During and after the implementation of general and complete disarmament, the most thorough control should be exer-

cised, the nature and extent of such control depending on the requirements for verification of the disarmament measures being carried out in each stage. To implement control over the inspection of disarmament, an international disarmament organization including all parties to the agreement should be created within the framework of the United Nations. This international disarmament organization and its inspectors should be assured unrestricted access without veto to all places as necessary for the purpose of effective verification.

7. Progress in disarmament should be accompanied by measures to strengthen institutions for maintaining peace and the settlement of international disputes by peaceful means. During and after the implementation of the programme of general and complete disarmament, there should be taken, in accordance with the principles of the United Nations Charter, the necessary measures to maintain international peace and security, including the obligation of States to place at the disposal of the United Nations agreed manpower necessary for an international peace force to be equipped with agreed types of armaments. Arrangements for the use of this force should ensure that the United Nations can effectively deter or suppress any threat or use of arms in violation of the purposes and principles of the United Nations.

8. States participating in the negotiations should seek to achieve and implement the widest possible agreement at the earliest possible date. Efforts should continue without interruption until agreement upon the total programme has been achieved, and efforts to ensure early agreement on and implementation of measures of disarmament should be undertaken without prejudicing progress on agreement on the total programme and in such a way that those measures would facilitate and form part of that programme.

Annex III

Treaty on the Nonproliferation of Nuclear Weapons, July 1, 1968

The States concluding this Treaty, hereinafter referred to as the "Parties to the Treaty",

Considering the devastation that would be visited upon all mankind by a nuclear war and the consequent need to make every effort to avert the danger of such a war and to take measures to safeguard the security of peoples,

Believing that the proliferation of nuclear weapons would seriously enhance the danger of nuclear war,

In conformity with resolutions of the United Nations General Assembly calling for the conclusion of an agreement on the prevention of wider dissemination of nuclear weapons,

Undertaking to cooperate in facilitating the application of International Atomic Energy Agency safeguards on peaceful nuclear activities,

Expressing their support for research, development and other efforts to further the application, within the framework of the International Atomic Energy safeguards system, of the principle of safeguarding effectively the flow of source and special fissionable materials by use of instruments and other techniques at certain strategic points,

Affirming the principle that the benefits of peaceful applications of nuclear technology, including any technological by-products which may be derived by nuclear-weapon States from the development of nuclear explosive devices, should be available for peaceful purposes to all Parties to the Treaty, whether nuclear-weapon or non-nuclear-weapon States,

Convinced that, in furtherance of this principle, all Parties to the Treaty are entitled to participate in the fullest possible exchange of scientific information for, and to contribute alone or in cooperation with other States to, the further development of the applications of atomic energy for peaceful purposes,

Declaring their intention to achieve at the earliest possible date the cessation of the nuclear arms race and to undertake effective measures in the direction of nuclear disarmament,

Urging the cooperation of all States in the attainment of this objective,

Recalling the determination expressed by the Parties to the 1963 Treaty banning nuclear weapon tests in the atmosphere in outer space and under water in its Preamble to seek to achieve the discontinuance of all test explosions of nuclear weapons for all time and to continue negotiations to this end,

Desiring to further the easing of international tension and the strengthening of trust between States in order to facilitate the cessation of the manufacture of nuclear weapons, the liquidation of all their existing stockpiles, and the elimination from national arsenals of nuclear weapons and the means of their delivery pursuant to a treaty on general and complete disarmament under strict and effective international control,

Recalling that, in accordance with the Charter of the United Nations, States must refrain in their international relations from the threat or use of force against the territorial integrity or political independence of any Sate, or in any other manner inconsistent with the Purposes of the United Nations, and that the establishment and maintenance of international peace and security are to be promoted with the least diversion for armaments of the world's human and economic resources,

Have agreed as follows:

ARTICLE I

Each nuclear-weapon State Party to the Treaty undertakes not to transfer to any recipient whatsoever nuclear weapons or other nuclear explosive devices or control over such weapons or explosive devices directly, or indirectly; and not in any way to assist, encourage, or acquire nuclear weapons or other nuclear explosive devices, or control over such weapons or explosive devices.

ARTICLE II

Each non-nuclear-weapon State Party to the Treaty undertakes not to receive the transfer from any transferor whatsoever of nuclear weapons or other nuclear explosive devices or of control over such weapons or explosive devices directly, or indirectly; not to manufacture or otherwise acquire nuclear weapons or other nuclear explosive devices; and not to seek or receive any assistance in the manufacture of nuclear weapons or other nuclear explosive devices.

ARTICLE III

1. Each non-nuclear-weapon State Party to the Treaty undertakes to accept safeguards, as set forth in an agreement to be negotiated and concluded with the International Atomic Energy Agency in accordance with the Statute of the International Atomic Energy Agency and the Agency's safeguards system, for the exclusive purpose of verification of the fulfillment of its obligations assumed under this Treaty with a view to preventing diversion of nuclear energy from peaceful uses to nuclear weapons or other nuclear explosive devices. Procedures for the safeguards required by this article shall be followed with respect to source or special fissionable material in all peaceful nuclear activities within the territory of such State, under its jurisdiction, or carried out under its control anywhere.

2. Each State Party to the Treaty undertakes not to provide: (a) source or special fissionable material, or (b) equipment or material especially designed or prepared for the processing, use or production of special fissionable material, to any non-nuclear-weapon State for peaceful purposes, unless the source or special fissionable material shall be subject to the safeguards required by this article.

3. The safeguards required by this article shall be implemented in a manner designed to comply with article IV of this Treaty, and

to avoid hampering the economic or technological development of the Parties or international cooperation in the field of peaceful nuclear activities, including the international exchange of nuclear material and equipment for the processing, use or production of nuclear material for peaceful purposes in accordance with the provisions of this article and the principle of safeguarding set forth in the Preamble of the Treaty.

4. Non-nuclear-weapon States Party to the Treaty shall conclude agreements with the International Atomic Energy Agency to meet the requirements of this article either individually or together with other States in accordance with the Statute of the International Atomic Energy Agency. Negotiations of such agreements shall commence within 180 days from the original entry into force of this Treaty. For States depositing their instruments of ratification or accession after the 180-day period, negotiation of such agreements shall commence not later than the date of such deposit. Such agreements shall enter into force not later than eighteen months after the date of initiation of negotiations.

ARTICLE IV

1. Nothing in this Treaty shall be interpreted as affecting the inalienable right of all the Parties to the Treaty to develop research, production and use of nuclear energy for peaceful purposes without discrimination and in conformity with articles I and II of this Treaty.

2. All the Parties of the Treaty undertake to facilitate, and have the right to participate in, the fullest possible exchange of equipment, materials and scientific and technological information for the peaceful uses of nuclear energy. Parties to the Treaty in a position to do so shall also cooperate in contributing alone or together with other States or international organizations to the further development of the applications of nuclear energy for peaceful purposes, especially in the territories of non-nuclear-weapon States Party to the Treaty, with due consideration for the needs of the developing areas of the world.

ARTICLE V

Each Party to the Treaty undertakes to take appropriate measures to ensure that, in accordance with this Treaty, under appropriate international observation and through appropriate international procedures, potential benefits from any peaceful applications of nuclear explosions will be made available to non-nuclear-weapon States Party to the Treaty on a nondiscriminatory basis and that the charge to such Parties for the explosive devices used will be as low as possible and exclude any charge for research and development, non-nuclear-weapon States Party to the Treaty shall be able to obtain such benefits, pursuant to a special international agreement or agreements, through an appropriate international body with adequate representation of non-nuclear-weapon States. Negotiations on this subject shall commence as soon as possible after the Treaty enters into force. Non-nuclear-weapon States Party to the Treaty so desiring may also obtain such benefits pursuant to bilateral agreements.

ARTICLE VI

Each of the Parties to the Treaty undertakes to pursue negotiations in good faith on effective measures relating to cessation of the nuclear arms race at an early date and to nuclear disarmament, and on a treaty on general and complete disarmament under strict and effective international control.

ARTICLE VII

Nothing in this Treaty affects the right of any group of States to conclude regional treaties in order to assure the total absence of nuclear weapons in their respective territories.

ARTICLE VIII

1. Any Party to the Treaty may purpose amendments to this Treaty. The text of any proposed amendment shall be submitted to

the Depositary Governments which shall circulate it to all Parties to the Treaty. Thereupon, if requested to do so by one-third or more of the Parties to the Treaty, the Depositary Governments shall convene a conference, to which they shall invite all the Parties to the Treaty, to consider such an amendment.

2. Any amendment to this Treaty must be approved by a majority of the votes of all the Parties to the Treaty, including the votes of all nuclear-weapon States Party to the Treaty and all other Parties which, on the date the amendment is circulated, are members of the Board of Governors of the International Atomic Energy Agency. The amendment shall enter into force for each Party that deposits its instrument of ratification of all nuclear-weapon States Party to the Treaty and all other Parties which, on the date the amendment is circulated, are members of the Board of Governors of the International Atomic Energy Agency. Thereafter, it shall enter into force for any other Party upon the deposit of its instrument of ratification of the amendment.

3. Five years after the entry into force of this Treaty, a conference of Parties to the Treaty shall be held in Geneva, Switzerland, in order to review the operation of this Treaty with a view to assuring that the purposes of the Preamble and the provisions of the Treaty are being realized. At intervals of five years thereafter, a majority of the Parties to the Treaty may obtain, by submitting a proposal to this effect to the Depositary Governments, the convening of further conferences with the same objective of reviewing the operation of the Treaty.

ARTICLE IX

1. This Treaty shall be open to all States for signature. Any State which does not sign the Treaty before its entry into force in accordance with paragraph 3 of this article may accede to it at any time.

2. This Treaty shall be subject to ratification by signatory States. Instruments of ratification and instruments of accession shall be deposited with the Governments of the United States of America,

the United Kingdom of Great Britain and Northern Ireland and the Union of Soviet Socialist Republics, which are hereby designated the Depositary Governments.

3. This Treaty shall enter into force after its ratification by the States, the Governments of which are designated Depositaries of the Treaty, and forty other States signatory to this Treaty and the deposit of their instruments of ratification. For the purposes of this Treaty, a nuclear-weapon State is one which has manufactured and exploded a nuclear weapon or other nuclear explosive device prior to January 1, 1967.

4. For States whose instruments of ratification or accession are deposited subsequent to the entry into force of this Treaty, it shall enter into force on the date of the deposit of their instruments of ratification or accession.

5. The Depositary Governments shall promptly inform all signatory and acceding States of the date of each signature, the date of deposit of each instrument of ratification or of accession, the date of the entry into force of this Treaty, and the date of receipt of any requests for convening a conference or other notices.

6. This Treaty shall be registered by the Depositary Governments pursuant to article 102 of the Charter of the United Nations.

ARTICLE X

1. Each Party shall in exercising its national sovereignty have the right to withdraw from the Treaty if it decides that extraordinary events, related to the subject matter of this Treaty, have jeopardized the supreme interests of its country. It shall give notice of such withdrawal to all other Parties to the Treaty and to the United Nations Security Council three months in advance. Such notice shall include a statement of the extraordinary events it regards as having jeopardized its supreme interests.

2. Twenty-five years after the entry into force of the Treaty, a conference shall be convened to decide whether the Treaty shall

continue in force indefinitely, or shall be extended for an additional fixed period or periods. This decision shall be taken by a majority of the Parties to the Treaty.

Article XI

This Treaty, the English, Russian, Spanish and Chinese texts of which are equally authentic, shall be deposited in the archives of the Depositary Governments. Duly certified copies of this Treaty shall be transmitted by the Depositary Governments to the Governments of the signatory and acceding States.

In witness whereof the undersigned, duly authorized, have signed this Treaty.

Done in triplicate, at the cities of Washington, London and Moscow, this first day of July one thousand nine hundred sixty-eight.

Annex IV

List of Photos

1. The mushroom cloud at Alamagordo, New Mexico. 16 July 1945.
2. Opening meeting of 1st Session of the General Assembly, London, (Attlee) (1946)
3. First Meeting of the Security Council, London, (1946)
4. Meeting of Security Council, 4 February 1946 (Vishinsky, Bevin, Stettinius, Lie) (1946)
5. First Meeting of United Nations Atomic Energy Commission, New York, (Baruch) (1946)
6. Eisenhower addressing the General Assembly, (Atoms for Peace) (1953)
7. Secretary-General Dag Hammarskjold at a meeting of the Tripartite Conference on the Discontinuance of Nuclear Weapon Tests, Geneva, (1959)
8. Khruschev addressing the General Assembly, (General and Complete Disarmament) (1959)
9. McCloy & Zorin, (Agreed Principles) (1961)
10. First Meeting of the Eighteen Nation Disarmament Committee (ENDC), Geneva, (1962)
11. General Burns with Barrington and Epstein (proposal for partial test ban in 1st Committee) (1962)
12. Signing the Partial Test Ban Treaty in Moscow (1963)
13. President Kennedy ratifies the Partial Test Ban Treaty, Washington, (1963)
14. Ambassador Alfonso Garcia Robles opening the 1965 session of the Preparatory Committee for the Denuclearization of Latin America (COPREDAL), Mexico, (1965)
15. Final meeting of COPREDAL for signing of Treaty of Tlatelolco
16. Alfonso Garcia Robles signing Treaty of Tlatelolco
17. Opening meeting of the 1966 session of the ENDC, Geneva, (1966)
18. Signing the Outer Space Treaty in Washington (1967)
19. Signing the Non-Proliferation Treaty on 1 July 1968, Washington, (1968)
20. Secretary-General U Thant addresses the Conference of the Committee on Disarmament, Geneva, (1970)

21. Signing the SALT I Agreements in Moscow (Nixon and Brezhnev) (1972)

22. The 1st Special Session of the General Assembly on Disarmament (1978)

23. Signing the SALT II Treaty in Vienna (Carter and Brezhnev) (1979)

24. Vice-President George Bush introduces the U.S. Draft Convention on the Prohibition of Chemical Weapons at the CD, Geneva (1984)

25. Signing the Treaty of Rarotonga, Cook Islands, (1985)

26. The First Summit Meeting of Gorbachev and Reagan in Geneva (1985)

27. Gorbachev and Reagan signing the Intermediate Nuclear Forces (INF) Treaty in Washington (1987)

28. Gorbachev and Reagan signing the Ratification of the INF Treaty in Moscow (1988)

29. The sculpture "Good Defeats Evil" (1990)

30. Opening Session of the Amendment Conference of the Partial Test Ban Treaty (1991)

31. Signing the START I Treaty by Gorbachev and Bush, Moscow, (1991)

32. The First Summit Meeting of the Security Council (1992)

33. Signing the START II Treaty (Yeltsin and Bush), Moscow, (1993)

34. Signing the Chemical Weapons Convention, Paris, (1993)

35. Opening Meeting of the Non-Proliferation Review and Extension Conference (1995)

36. Signing the Treaty of Bangkok, (1995)

37. Signing the Treaty of Pelindaba (South Africa), Cairo, (1996)

38. Advisory Opinion of the International Court of Justice, The Hague, (1996)

39. Opening of the General Assembly meeting on 9 September 1996. Ambassador Richard Butler of Australia introducing the resolution to adopt the Comprehensive Nuclear Test Ban Treaty. (CTBT)

40. Signing the CTBT by President Clinton at the United Nations (1996)

In addition to the photographs, the exhibition includes a map of the world showing the increasing extent of nuclear weapon-free-zones.

Note on the Author

William Epstein, Chairman of the Editorial Board of *Disarmament Times*, was for many years Director of Disarmament in the U.N. Secretariat. He represented the Secretary-General at the negotiations at the Conference of Disarmament in Geneva, and its predecessor, the Eighteen Nation Disarmament Committee, from 1962 to 1973. Their work led to the Partial Test Ban Treaty (1963), the Nuclear Non-Proliferation Treaty (1968), the Seabed Arms Control Treaty (1971), and the Biological Weapons Convention (1972). He has attended all five review conferences of the Non-Proliferation Treaty as well as the 1995 extension conference.

He also represented the Secretary-General at the Commission for the Denuclearization of Latin America in Mexico City from 1965 to 1967. As Technical Consultant to the Commission, he prepared, at the request of its Chairman, Alfonso Garcia Robles, 1982 Nobel Peace Prize laureate, the first draft of the text which became the 1967 Treaty of Tlatelolco creating a Nuclear-Free Zone in Latin America and the Caribbean.

He has authored a number of books, including *The Last Chance: Nuclear Proliferation and Arms Control*, a standard reference work, and *The Prevention of Nuclear War: A United Nations Perspective*, and has published more than 300 articles on disarmament and international security.

He was a member of the Canadian Delegation to six sessions of the U.N. General Assembly.

He is the only person who has been at the United Nations for its entire first half century. He has been involved in disarmament efforts in an official capacity for 50 years, longer than any person alive.

He represents the Pugwash Conferences on Science and World Affairs at the U.N., where that organization has official NGO status, and attended the Nobel Peace Prize Award to Joseph Rotblat and Pugwash in Oslo on December 10, 1995.

كيفية الحصول على منشورات الأمم المتحدة

يمكن الحصول على منشورات الأمم المتحدة من المكتبات ودور التوزيع في جميع أنحاء العالم . استعلم عنها من المكتبة
التي تتعامل معها أو اكتب إلى : الأمم المتحدة . قسم البيع في نيويورك أو في جنيف .

如何购取联合国出版物

联合国出版物在全世界各地的书店和经售处均有发售。请向书店询问或写信到纽约或日内瓦的
联合国销售组。

HOW TO OBTAIN UNITED NATIONS PUBLICATIONS

United Nations publications may be obtained from bookstores and distributors throughout the
world. Consult your bookstore or write to: United Nations, Sales Section, New York or Geneva.

COMMENT SE PROCURER LES PUBLICATIONS DES NATIONS UNIES

Les publications des Nations Unies sont en vente dans les librairies et les agences dépositaires
du monde entier. Informez-vous auprès de votre libraire ou adressez-vous à : Nations Unies,
Section des ventes, New York ou Genève.

КАК ПОЛУЧИТЬ ИЗДАНИЯ ОРГАНИЗАЦИИ ОБЪЕДИНЕННЫХ НАЦИЙ

Издания Организации Объединенных Наций можно купить в книжных магазинах
и агентствах во всех районах мира. Наводите справки об изданиях в вашем книжном
магазине или пишите по адресу: Организация Объединенных Наций, Секция по
продаже изданий, Нью-Йорк или Женева.

COMO CONSEGUIR PUBLICACIONES DE LAS NACIONES UNIDAS

Las publicaciones de las Naciones Unidas están en venta en librerías y casas distribuidoras en
todas partes del mundo. Consulte a su librero o diríjase a: Naciones Unidas, Sección de Ventas,
Nueva York o Ginebra.

Litho in United Nations, New York
22544—September 1997—6,670
ISBN 92-1-142224-8

United Nations publication
Sales No. E.97.IX.4